Akahime (red princess) costume worn by princesses and daughters of shoguns (paramount military chiefs) and daimyos (noblemen) in *jidaimono*.

Plate 1.

Yoshitsune (an 11th-century military leader)
in *Yoshitsune Sembonzakura*
(The Thousand Cherry Trees).
Jidaimono.

Plate 2.

Yugiri (a courtesan)
in *Kuruwa Bunsho*
(Tales of the Licensed Quarter).
Sewamono.

Plate 3.

Lady Iwafuji (a lady-in-waiting)
in *Kagamiyama Kokyo no Nishikie*
(The Women's Chushingura).
Jidaimono.

Plate 4.

Title role in *Uirouri*
(The Medicine Vendor).
Juhachiban.

Plate 5.

The ghost of General Tomomori
(11th-century figure) in *Funa Benkei*
(Benkei in the Boat).
Shosagoto.

Plate 6.

Ryujinmaki (ceremonial costume with stiff, standing right sleeve), worn in *jidaimono* by messengers attached to the nobility.

Plate 7.

Benkei (an 11th-century warrior)
in *Kanjincho (The Subscription List).*
Juhachiban.

Plate 8.

Miyokichi (a courtesan)
in *Meigetsu Hachiman Matsuri*
(The Full Moon on the Hachiman Festival).
Sewamono.

Plate 9.

Akuba costume
worn by villainous women
in *sewamono*.

Plate 10.

Warrior disguised as a servant in *Kamahige*
(*Shave with a Sickle*).
Juhachiban.

Plate 11.

Entrance costume of Hanako (a temple dancer)
in *Musume Dojoji*
(The Maiden at the Dojo Temple).
Shosagoto.

Plate 12.

Hanako in *Musume Dojoji*
(The Maiden at the Dojo Temple).
Shosagoto.

Plate 13.

The lion spirit in *Kagami Jishi*
(*The Dancing Lion*).
Shosagoto.

Plate 14.

Yayoi (a waiting-woman)
in *Kagami Jishi (The Dancing Lion)*.
Shosagoto.

Plate 15.

Umeomaru (retainer of a 9th-century privy councillor)
in *Sugawara Denju Tenarai Kagami*
(The Secret of Sugawara's Calligraphy).
Jidaimono.

Plate 16.